Hosannas to the King!

A Palm Sunday Suite for Organ

Mary McDonald

Editor: Douglas E. Wagner
Music Engraving: Linda Taylor
Cover Design: Patti Jeffers

ISBN: 978-1-4291-2999-2

Lorenz

A Lorenz Company • www.lorenz.com

Foreword

From the endless wellspring of her creative invention, composer Mary McDonald has penned for us this highly effective and wholly useful suite of hymn tune settings for Palm Sunday worship. A brilliant prelude on ST. THEODULPH, an embracing offertory on STORY OF JESUS, and a thrilling postlude on ELLACOMBE, all come together in presenting the organist with well-crafted and accessible choices for the three main instrumental elements of the service.

—The Publisher

Contents

All Glory, Laud, and Honor 3
    ST. THEODULPH

Tell Me the Story of Jesus 8
    STORY OF JESUS

Hosanna, Loud Hosanna 11
    ELLACOMBE

About this series

Sunday Suites are concise, practical books designed to provide church pianists and organists with quality arrangements for special days on the church calendar. Each *Sunday Suite* offers a prelude, offertory, and postlude (and sometimes one "bonus" piece) to cover the keyboardist's needs for a complete service. Watch for more *Sunday Suites*, written by some of your favorite Lorenz arrangers.

All Glory, Laud, and Honor

Sw. Foundations 8, 4
Gt. Foundations 8, 4, Light Mixture, Sw. to Gt.
Ch. Solo 8
Ped. 16, 8, 4, Gt. to Ped.

Mary McDonald
Tune: ST. THEODULPH
by **Melchior Teschner** (1584-1635)

Duration: 3:00

70/1821L-3

+ Trumpet 8

Tell Me the Story of Jesus

Sw.   Strings 8, 4, Flutes 8, Ch. to Sw.
Ch.   Strings 8, 4
Ped. Soft 16, 8

Mary McDonald
Tune: **STORY OF JESUS**
by **John R. Sweney** (1837-1899)

Duration: 2:45

Hosanna, Loud Hosanna

Sw. Bright Reed 8; Prepare: Strings and Flutes 8, 4
Gt. Foundations 8, 4, (2)
Ped. Foundations 16, 8, Bright Reed 8

Mary McDonald
Tune: **ELLACOMBE**
from "Gesangbuch der Herzogl," 1784

Duration: 3:30

Strings and Flutes 8, 4

16

70/1821L-16